focus on asia

Thailand

SCOTT BRODIE

CONTENTS

The Kingdom of Thailand

Copyright Trocadero Publishing

SCALE - KILOMETRES

0   300

VIETNAM

LAOS

BURMA

Chiang Mai

Lampang

Udon Thani

Sukhothai

Phitsanulok

Khon Kaen

Nakhon Sawan

Ayutthaya

Ubon
Ratchathani

Nakhon
Ratchasima

Thonburi   BANGKOK

CAMBODIA

ANDAMAN

SEA

GULF

OF

THAILAND

Nakhon Si Thammarat

Phuket

SOUTH

CHINA

SEA

MALAYSIA

Introduction to Thailand

Thailand is renowned around the world as a nation with a unique culture. It stands alone in Asia in that it was never colonised by the empires of Europe.

Millions of visitors flock there each year to sample its uniqueness, and invariably are welcomed generously by the friendly Thai people. Visitors enjoy a land of enormous contrasts, from the superb beaches to the dense rainforests and hill country.

Another special aspect of the nation is its deep reverence for the monarchy. King Bhumipol, the longest reigning monarch in the world, occupies an unchallenged position. The Chakri Dynasty, of which he is the ninth King, boasts many famous reformers.

At the other extreme, for seventy years Thailand has been notorious for unstable governments. From the 1950s to the 1990s the nation was tormented by a string of military-backed *coups d'état*. Also, corruption was rife within the governing parties.

The severe Asian economic slowdown of 1997–98 began in Thailand following the collapse of its currency. Since then the nation has worked hard, with considerable success, to rebuild its economy.

Thais are fiercely independent. They have their own unique language, both written and spoken, and their special version of Buddhism.

All these aspects combine to make Thailand one of the most interesting and intriguing countries in Asia.

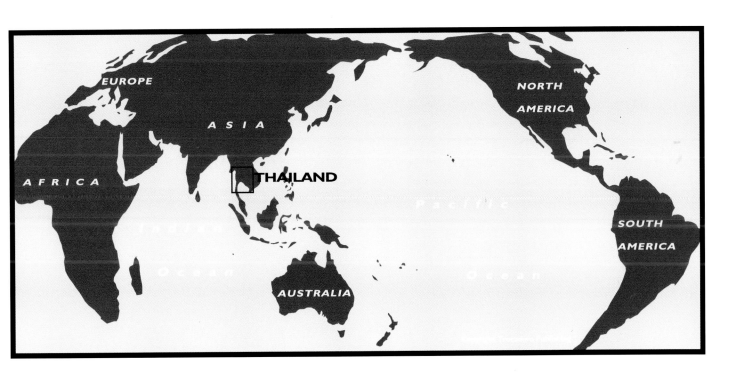

Government structure

The place of the king

King Bhumibol Adulyedej, Rama IX, is the most enduring and dominant figure in Thai society today. Born at Cambridge, Massachusetts, in the USA on 5 December 1927, he is the son of Prince Mahidol Adulyedej and Princess Phra Sringarindra Boromarajajonani. His elder brother was King Rama VIII, who died in 1946 in suspicious circumstances.

Bhumibol is the grandson of King Chulalongkorn (Rama V), renowned for the reforms he brought

Until 1932 Thailand was an absolute monarchy. The king was the government and appointed all civil servants and ministers. Reformists forced the monarch to adopt a system of government similar to those of European nations. The king became the symbolic head of state, while the people were able to elect a government led by a prime minister.

Although the kings maintained this position, the governments of Thailand proved to be erratic. In seventy years there has been a mixture of civilian and military governments and even a period under martial law. At various times the constitution has been abandoned or changed radically.

Today Thailand is once more under civilian rule, with an elected government led by a prime minister. The influence of the military on the government has been reduced.

SIAM OR THAILAND

Siam was the collective name given to Thailand by early European arrivals in the seventeenth century. By the nineteenth century it had entered standard usage as the name of the kingdom.

In 1939 the ultra-nationalistic Prime Minister Pribun Songkhran changed the name to Thailand. When he was deposed in 1945 the name Siam was reinstated. In 1948, when Pribun again assumed power, he changed the name for the last time.

King Bhumipol at the time of his coronation

to Thai society during his reign. His father, Prince Mahidol, was an enthusiastic scientist, the father of Thailand's modern medical profession.

After much time spent in Europe, Prince Mahidol and his family returned to Thailand in the 1920s. He died there in 1929 when Bhumibol was only two years old. The family left once again for Europe in the 1930s. His brother Ananda Mahidol was declared heir to the throne in 1935, at the age of ten. The family remained in Switzerland and a Council of Regents ruled in Thailand until Ananda was old enough to be crowned.

Bhumibol was educated at the École Nouvelle de la Suisse Romand and at Lausanne University in Switzerland. He was at school in Switzerland when his brother's death was revealed. Faced with the prospect of taking over as monarch, he abandoned the study of science at Lausanne University. In its place he chose a course of political science and law, to equip him for his new role. Remaining in Switzerland as a student, he returned to Thailand for his coronation as King Rama IX on 5 May 1950. After a further period of study in Switzerland, he finally returned permanently in 1951.

In 1949 he married Princess Rajawongse Sirikit. They have four children: Princess Ubol Ratana, Prince Maha Vajiralongkorn, Princess Maha Chakri Sirindhorn and Princess Chulabhorn. Maha Vajiralongkorn is heir to the throne, being the first-born male in the family. However, many Thais would prefer that Princess Ubol Ratana inherited the monarchy.

The role of King Bhumibol is now largely ceremonial. He applies the royal seal to legislation passed by the National Assembly and conducts the swearing-in of government ministers. He is also involved in projects all over Thailand that are aimed at improving the lot of the people.

While he has no legal powers, his influence is immense. His reign has greatly enhanced the stature of the monarchy, repairing the damage done during the 1930s and 1940s. Thais are deeply respectful of the King and are quick to anger at any disrespect shown to him. His influence was amply illustrated during the crisis of 1992.

www.sources
kanchanapisek.or.th/biography/index.en.html
The Golden Jubilee Network

www.palaces.thai.net/
Virtual tours of the royal palaces

Transport

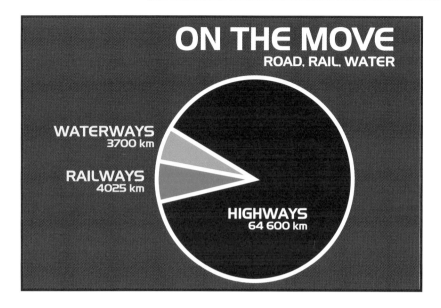

ON THE MOVE
ROAD, RAIL, WATER

WATERWAYS
3700 km

RAILWAYS
4025 km

HIGHWAYS
64 600 km

Public transport

Apart from the private motor car, there are many forms of transport for Thai people. The simplest and least polluting is the samlor, which means 'three wheels'. Samlors are similar to the trishaws or pedicabs found in other parts of Asia. The driver rides a bicycle to which is attached a small seat mounted on two wheels. For a small charge the driver takes a passenger to a destination. Samlors are most common in cities and towns outside Bangkok.

For the more daring, there is the motorcycle taxi. A small fare entitles the passenger to sit on the pillion of a motorcycle while the driver zips in and out of the heavy traffic. In places such as Bangkok, this is probably the most dangerous of all transport modes.

The best known form of transport in Thailand is the tuk tuk. These are three-wheeled vehicles — basically a motor scooter at the front, with an open canopied compartment at the back capable of taking two or three passengers. The streets of the cities are infested with tuk tuks. While they are a good, cheap form of transport, the drawback is the high level of pollution produced by their two-stroke engines.

For Thais the most popular form of transport is the bus. Buses operate commuter services all over Bangkok and in some cities outside the capital. Buses also operate long-distance services linking most parts of the kingdom. They range from the older, non-air-conditioned type that is very cheap to ride to the newer, air-conditioned variety that is becoming increasingly common on Bangkok streets. The back seat on all buses is where Buddhist monks sit. If a monk gets on a

A long-tail boat on the Chao Praya River

bus, Thais are expected to vacate one of the seats at the back.

Outside Bangkok, particularly in places like Chiang Mai, commuter services are provided by the song taew. This minibus is similar in some ways to the jeepney of Manila — a small truck with a cabin at the back in which passengers sit on flat board seats. Fares on song taews are low.

Fifty years ago Bangkok was a city made unique by the canals that criss-crossed it. These canals, or klongs, provided the primary form of transport, with specially developed narrow boats known as 'long tails' because of the propeller shaft extending from the engine. From the 1960s, as cars became predominant, many canals were filled in or covered over to create roadways. There are still some klongs today, and a few scheduled boat services using them. Express boats also operate along the Chao Praya River, with regular stops.

In Bangkok there are several modern, high-speed commuter rail services developed and owned by private companies. Prior to the economic slowdown in 1997–98 elaborate and expansive plans were made for lines running to all parts of Bangkok. These were dramatically scaled back when money became short.

Two lines opened in December 1999, but patronage has not been good. The main reason is the relatively high fares, which are beyond the reach of many Thais. The railway, known as Skytrain, runs on concrete viaducts above main roads.

Railways

In 1891, under the modernising reign of King Chulalongkorn, a British company was commissioned to construct a railway north from Bangkok. The first service departed the new Bangkok station on 26 March 1894, for a trip to Ayutthaya, inaugurating the Royal State Railways of Siam. As happened in

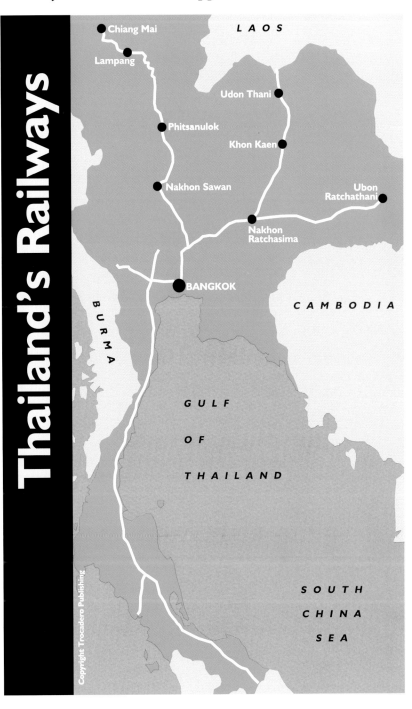

Thailand's Railways

Copyright Trocadero Publishing

SCOTT BRODIE

many parts of the world, separate railway lines were developed using different gauges. In 1920 a program was begun to alter all lines to the 1435 millimetre (4'8½" standard) gauge.

Tracks were built to many parts of the kingdom. By 1946 the total length was 2481 kilometres. During World War II the system was badly damaged by bombing and required considerable restoration work in the late 1940s. Railways of Thailand was formed in 1951, and further development brought the length of track to just over 4000 kilometres. Today the railways are the largest government-owned enterprise in Thailand, employing 26 000 people.

AIRPORTS

With paved runways	56
With unpaved runways	50

Road

Thailand is well known for its heavy traffic, especially in Bangkok. As the nation grew more affluent, the level of car ownership expanded. Unfortunately, much of the road system has not developed accordingly. There are a number of motorways, mostly toll roads, in Bangkok and its surrounds; however, cars and other vehicles still use a network of narrow streets that were not designed for motorised vehicles.

The traffic jams of Bangkok are notorious around the world. During the 1990s some concerted efforts were made to improve the situation and things have improved. A program of building more toll roads and overpasses has helped ease the congestion, but there is not enough emphasis on creating better conditions for public transport. The exhaust emissions of vehicles stalled in traffic jams remains one of Thailand's worst sources of air pollution.

Aviation

Thailand has an extensive domestic airline network. Thai Airways is the major domestic carrier, serving twenty destinations, with Bangkok Airways also operating some services within Thailand. Given the difficulties of travelling by road and the slowness of the railways, air travel is usually the fastest method of getting around the kingdom.

Bangkok is a major tourist destination for the world, and attracts many business travellers. Bangkok is also an important airline hub for eastern Asia, with a large number of international carriers flying to Don Muang Airport. Thai Airways schedules hundreds of international flights to all parts of Asia and other continents, serving fifty destinations. The airline was established in the 1960s with technical assistance from Scandinavian Airlines System (SAS).

Shipping

Thailand is a major manufacturing country, with a huge volume of exports being shipped off daily to markets in North America, Europe and other destinations. Thus, ocean shipping plays a major part in the commercial life of the country. To further develop its standards, the Thai Port Authority has an agreement with the Port of London to obtain technical and operational expertise.

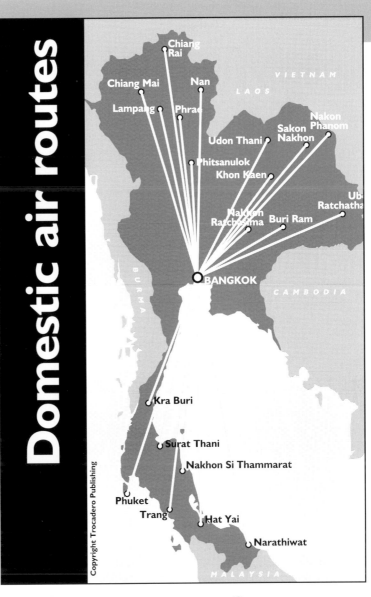

Domestic air routes

Copyright Trocadero Publishing

There are two main ports: Bangkok and Laem Chabang. The port of Bangkok, at the mouth of the Chao Praya River, is a major point of arrival and departure for cargo, processing 6.7 million tonnes and 534 000 containers per year. Laem Chabang is even larger, processing 950 000 tonnes in 995 000 containers.

Thailand's shipping fleet

Bulk ships 39
Cargo ships 135
Chemical tankers 3
Combination bulk ships 1
Container ships 13
Liquefied gas tankers 19
Multi-functional large load carriers 3
Passenger ships 1
Petroleum tankers 63
Refrigerated cargo ships 13
Roll-on roll-off ships 2
Short-sea passenger ships 2
Specialised tankers 5

Communications

Thailand's telephone system is mainly the traditional multichannel cable and microwave radio relay variety. A domestic satellite system is under development to speed the penetration of services into more remote regions.

Telephone ownership and usage are quite common among residents of Bangkok; however, there are many people in provincial areas for whom telephones play very little part in daily life. While only one person in twenty has a mobile or cellular telephone, ownership is growing rapidly, particularly when the conventional cable telephone system cannot meet the demand.

Thailand is well served by both television and radio. There are more than 200 AM band radio stations, and around 350 on the FM band. Ownership of radio receivers is widespread, with around 14 million in use. Audio broadcasts are a primary source of information and entertainment for the population, especially in the provinces.

Thailand's five television networks are all based in Bangkok; however, they each have repeater stations located strategically throughout the kingdom. Programming is a mixture of locally produced drama, comedy and current affairs, as well as programs imported from other countries. Around 16 million television receivers are in use in Thai homes.

The internet is freely available, but home computer ownership is not common. This limits access to the

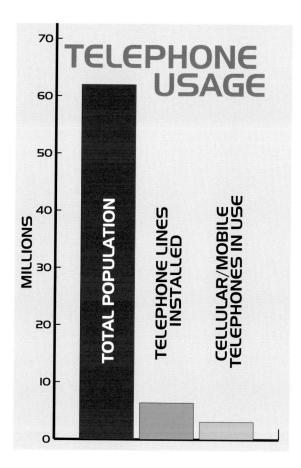

more affluent members of the community, though internet cafes are very popular with younger Thais.

Newspapers in Thailand are fiercely independent and very outspoken. As well as the major Thai language dailies, there are two highly respected English language newspapers: the *Bangkok Post* and *The Nation*. Because of restrictions on press freedoms in many parts of Asia, Thailand's newspapers are often taken as an indicator of thinking in the region.

WWW.SOURCES

www.newsdirectory.com/news/press/as/th/
Thai newspaper sites

www.inet.co.th/it-week/tat.htm
Telecommunications Association of Thailand

Industry: primary and secondary

Thailand has a strong primary industry sector. More than half the population is involved in agricultural production; however, a large portion of this is at village subsistence level. For more than a century Thailand has been able to meet all its own needs in rice production, as well as being a major exporter of the commodity. It also sends its rubber, sugar, corn and other products to world markets.

Since World War II, successive Thai governments have promoted the development of secondary industries

EXPORTS
WHERE THAILAND SENDS ITS EXPORTS

GERMANY
TAIWAN
CHINA
MALAYSIA
UK
NETHERLANDS
HONG KONG
SINGAPORE

OTHERS

USA

JAPAN

THAILAND'S PRINCIPAL CROPS
rice, cassava (tapioca), rubber, corn,
sugar cane, coconuts, soybeans

that earn export sales for the nation. Initially these were centred on footwear, clothing and associated products. In more recent times, high-technology production has enabled Thailand to become a major centre for the manufacture of electronic equipment such as computers, computer components and domestic appliances.

Thailand is one of the world's most popular destinations for tourists. The relaxed Thai lifestyle and unique culture, free from any colonial influences,

Many multinational corporations
have major presences in Thailand

SCOTT BRODIE

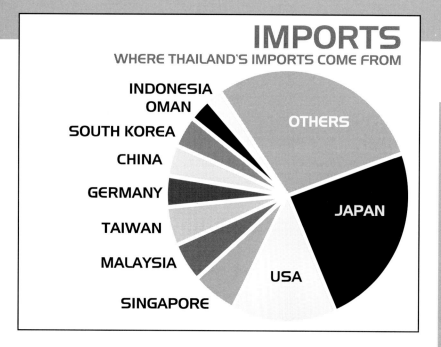

IMPORTS
WHERE THAILAND'S IMPORTS COME FROM

INDONESIA
OMAN
SOUTH KOREA
CHINA
GERMANY
TAIWAN
MALAYSIA
SINGAPORE
OTHERS
JAPAN
USA

is a magnet for people from all over the world. As well as the culture, the environment is a major drawcard. Visitors range through all parts of the country, from the superb beaches in the south to the jungles and hill country of the north. Tourism earns vast amounts of foreign currency for Thailand; however, it has been affected by the worldwide slump caused by the terrorist acts of 11 September 2001 and the subsequent military actions.

Following the economic collapse of 1997, a major recovery plan was put in place by the Thai government in cooperation with the International Monetary Fund. The manner in which all Thais tackled the economic problems saw the kingdom's position improve substantially, to the point where healthy growth has recommenced.

THAILAND'S EXPORTS
US$58.5 billion

Main exports
Computers and components, clothing and textiles, rice

THAILAND'S IMPORTS
US$45 billion

Main imports
Capital goods, intermediate goods and raw materials, consumer goods, fuels

WWW.sources
www.exportsthailand.com/
Exports from Thailand

www.mahidol.ac.th/Thailand/economy/manufac-sec.html
Summary of manufacturing in Thailand

www.doa.go.th/home/OI.html
Department of Agriculture

Geography, environment and climate

country extending down the Malay Peninsula.

Geographically, Thailand has four distinct areas: north-east, north, central and south. The north, marked by its deep valleys and heavily forested regions, is located in the lower foothills of the Himalayas. The north-east is a semi-arid plateau region best suited

Life goes on for most Thais even when the streets are flooded after a heavy tropical downpour

T hailand covers an area of around 513 000 square kilometres, roughly the size of France. In the north it is landlocked on three sides, having borders with Burma in the north-west, Laos in the north-east and Cambodia in the east. To the south it fronts on to the Gulf of Thailand on the eastern side and the Andaman Sea on the western side. There is a long narrow strip of

to grazing animals. Central is the mainly flat and highly fertile region around the Chao Praya River, which flows south through Bangkok and empties into the Gulf of Thailand. South is the long thin strip on the isthmus connecting the Malay Peninsula to Asia.

THAILAND'S SIZE
Area 514 000 sq. km
Land borders 4863 km   Coastline 3219 km

THAILAND'S LAND USE

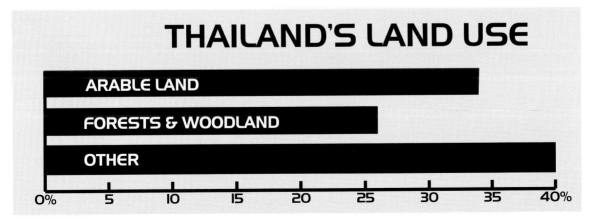

| ARABLE LAND |
| FORESTS & WOODLAND |
| OTHER |

0%   5   10   15   20   25   30   35   40%

Thailand's geography

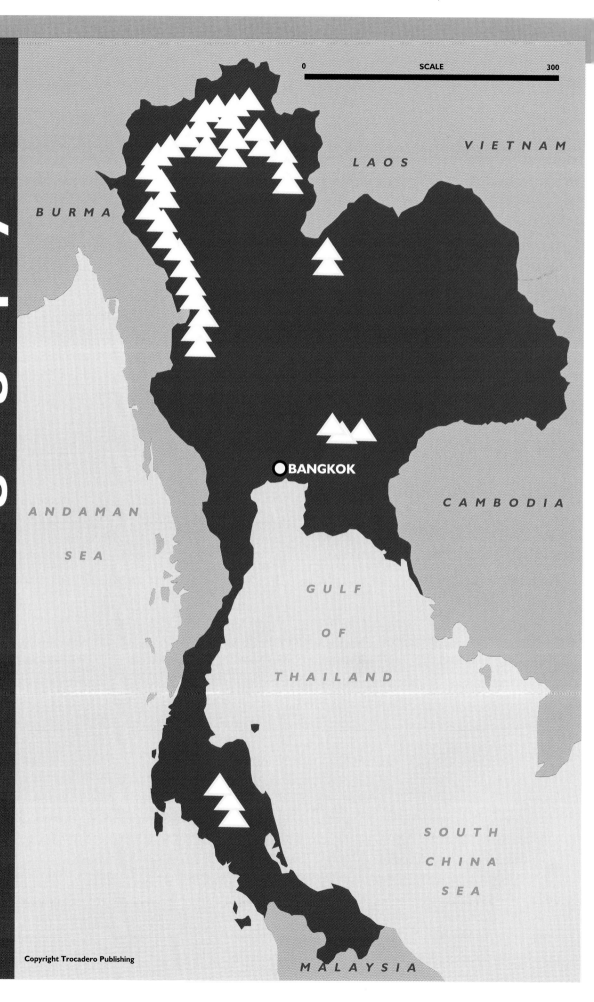

SCALE

0   300

VIETNAM

LAOS

BURMA

BANGKOK

ANDAMAN

SEA

CAMBODIA

GULF

OF

THAILAND

SOUTH

CHINA

SEA

MALAYSIA

Thailand's climate is tropical, with some months of the year experiencing heavy rainfall and intense humidity. The average temperatures through the year range from 20°C to 37°C. Such conditions contribute greatly to the fertility of the country, enabling it to cultivate a wide range of tropical crops.

There are three distinct seasons each year: rainy, cool, and hot. The

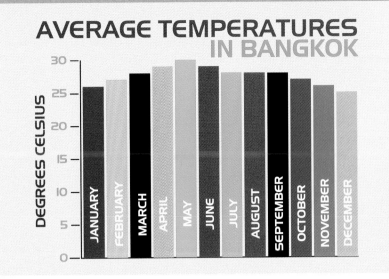

AVERAGE TEMPERATURES
IN BANGKOK

DEGREES CELSIUS

JANUARY · FEBRUARY · MARCH · APRIL · MAY · JUNE · JULY · AUGUST · SEPTEMBER · OCTOBER · NOVEMBER · DECEMBER

Monsoon
from the Arabic word
mawsin, or season

rainy season extends from June to October and is marked by the arrival of the south-west monsoon, which brings heavy rain most days, interspersed with intense sunshine. This is the most humid and uncomfortable time of year. It is also the time when sudden downpours flood the streets and roads, throwing cities like Bangkok into chaos. Between November and February is the coolest and driest time of year. The hot season, which arrives in March and departs in May, is when the schools take a two-month break.

In cities such as Bangkok, intense traffic congestion means severe exhaust emission pollution levels in the atmosphere. There are also major problems with water pollution caused by inadequate sewerage systems and discharges from factories. Overuse of agricultural land has led to soil erosion and severe deforestation. Some of the unique wildlife of the jungles has been affected by illegal hunting and trapping.

SCOTT BRODIE

Religion and beliefs

Buddhism is at the core of Thai life, with all but five per cent of the population being Buddhist. The faith began with Siddhartha Gautama, who lived in India 2500 years ago. He taught people to follow the Middle Path between the two extremes of great luxury and great hardship. Followers were encouraged to overcome greed and desire to lead wiser, more caring lives.

Buddhism made its way into Thai society from India around 2000 years ago. However, it was the greatest of the Sukhothai kings, Ramkamhaeng, who was crowned in 1279, who

The Wat Phra Keo houses the holy Emerald Buddha

A richly decorated Buddhist temple

Thailand is dotted with many small Buddhist shrines such as this one, the famous Erawan Shrine in central Bangkok

formalised Buddhism in the thirteenth century. He introduced the Therava form of Buddhism from Ceylon (Sri Lanka). Royal patronage ensured its adoption throughout the kingdom.

While Buddhism is predominant, there is no restriction on other religions being practised in Thailand. The most common forms other than Buddhism are Islam, Christianity and Hinduism.

Worship is an individual matter. Many people have shrines and Buddha images in their homes, and also visit temples to make offerings and hear sermons on important dates. Young men commonly become monks for a brief period, usually following the death of a grandfather. Buddhist monks are greatly revered in Thai society.

RELIGIOUS FAITHS

OTHERS

BUDDHIST

www.sources
www.mahidol.ac.th/Thailand/religion/r_buddhi.html
History of Buddhism in Thailand
www.inthai.org/thailand/religion.htm
Information on Thai Buddhism

Peoples and daily life

It is believed the human habitation of Thailand goes back at least 10 000 years. Finds by archaeological expeditions indicate a primitive cave-dwelling culture existed around that time. The first identifiable culture is that of the Negrito, who were followed by the Mon-Khmer and the Lawa. The Mon eventually migrated westward to the Salween River region, while the Khmers went east, forming the basis of Cambodia. The Lawa tended to spread in a north–south direction in mid-Thailand.

About 2300 years ago migration from India had a profound effect on these peoples. All three groups gradually adopted Indian religious and cultural ways. From this source came Buddhism, which, after various modifications, has become the dominant religion of Thailand. The next influence came from the north-east, as Chinese began migrating into the region.

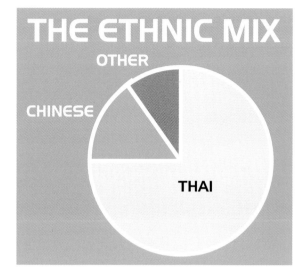

THE ETHNIC MIX

OTHER

CHINESE

THAI

The Thai language is complicated, with an eighty-letter alphabet and continuous running script without breaks. Thai speech is also complicated, with five different tones that need to be spoken correctly or words will mean something different from what the speaker intended.

Daily life for Thai people varies enormously depending on which part of the country you are in. For people in rural regions it is long working days, from sunrise to sunset, engaging in agriculture, cultivating crops. Whole families are involved in the maintenance of a farm, with children taking part in the activities before and after attending school.

In the cities, particularly Bangkok, people working in offices or factories begin work around 8.00 am, finishing in the early evening. The hardest or most frustrating part of the day for many is the journey to and from work. Heavy traffic congestion means it often takes up to two hours to get from home to work, and another two hours to get home again.

Houses on the Chao Praya River

SCOTT BRODIE

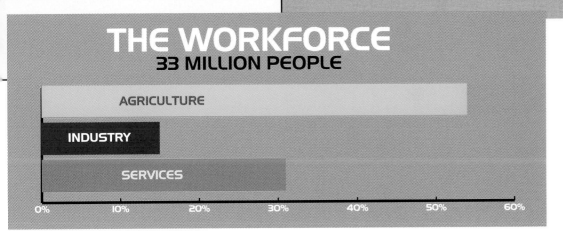

THE WORKFORCE
33 MILLION PEOPLE

AGRICULTURE

INDUSTRY

SERVICES

0%   10%   20%   30%   40%   50%   60%

Workplaces vary greatly, from simple family-owned factories or shops with minimal facilities to large modern offices and factories with better working conditions and air-conditioned premises.

Recreation in the cities takes a number of forms. The Thai people are mostly gregarious, enjoying socialising in small or large groups. This often takes the form of gathering to eat, with friends or in family groups, at home or in cafés or restaurants.

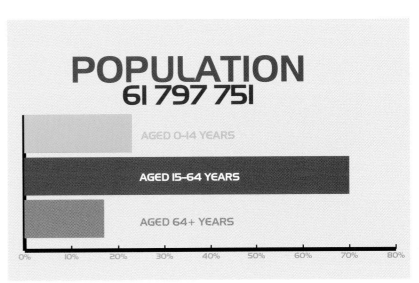

POPULATION
61 797 751

AGED 0–14 YEARS

AGED 15–64 YEARS

AGED 64+ YEARS

0%   10%   20%   30%   40%   50%   60%   70%   80%

Restaurants featuring Thai food are found everywhere; however, Western-style fast-food outlets are also growing in popularity. Thais are also enthusiastic film-goers. Spectator sports of all kinds are popular, with Thai kick-boxing, in particular, attracting large crowds.

Enjoying fresh coconut milk at a roadside stall

WWW.SOURCES
www.mahidol.ac.th/Thailand/glance-thai/culture.html
Thai culture and peoples

www.asiadragons.com/thailand/arts_and_culture/
Links to many websites on Thai culture

LONELY PLANET IMAGES — JOHN HAY

Part of a mural depicting scenes from the *Ramakian*, Thailand's version of the Indian Ramayana story

Arts, crafts and li

Music

Thai music has a lot in common with that of China. It features a unique diatonic structure unlike any European musical style. Also, unlike the West, there is no heritage of religious music, as it has never been a part of Buddhist worship. Previously discouraged by monks, some forms of music are now permitted as part of ceremonies on special festive occasions.

Drama and dance

Traditional Thai drama and dance trace their origins back to India. Performances were originally linked closely to Buddhism and could only be witnessed in monasteries on special occasions. The slow, graceful style and movements are called lakhon. Over the centuries, the style of performance has evolved and been refined and today has even taken on some Western influences.

Architecture

As in Europe, the early Thai architectural style derived from religious requirements. Temple design owed a great deal to Chinese architecture, although influences such as the tapering tiered roof came from Cambodia. Fine examples of Thai architecture can be seen in Bangkok's Grand Palace complex. Modern Thai architecture tends to follow the Western style, at least for commercial buildings, although even these usually have distinctive Thai flourishes.

Painting

Early Thai painting, with its own distinctive style, was mostly found within temples. It usually took the form of continuous wall murals that told a story. Modern Thai painting has taken up Western styles to a large degree, but retains typically Thai influences.

A traditional theatrical troupe in the early twentieth century

ture

Thai dancers maintain the tradition that began in Buddhist celebrations

Literature

While Thai literature can be traced back to the thirteenth century, the ravages of the climate mean few original works have survived. Influenced by Buddhism, the original writings were records of stories, legends and history previously passed from person to person by word of mouth.

As the tradition developed, less emphasis was placed on using writing to further Buddhism and more on recording history and relating stories. *The Ramayana* from India was translated into Thai, as were portions of *The Mahabharata.*

During the twentieth century translations of popular Chinese historical romances became very popular in Thailand. Today Thai writings mingle with literature from around the world that has been translated into Thai.

Crafts

Thailand's unique crafts have been developed over centuries. The strongest Thai influences can be seen in baskets, textiles, earthenware, lacquer work, wood carvings and altar tables. All are distinctively Thai and much admired around the world. There is also a thriving culture of creating theatrical masks, puppets and costumes for drama and dance.

Food and cuisine

The cuisine of Thailand is famous and much loved around the world. Like most things Thai, it is unique, despite being a centuries-old blending of both Eastern and Western cooking styles. The Buddhist faith does not encourage large pieces of meat in meals, so most meat-based dishes feature meats shredded to a small size and mixed with herbs and spices.

The original Thai cuisine was designed to suit a waterborne lifestyle, but this gradually changed. At first stewing, baking and grilling were the most common cooking methods; however, growing Chinese influences on Thai culture saw the introduction of stir-frying.

The coming of Europeans from the late 1500s brought new influences to the Thai cuisine. While chilli is today seen as a core ingredient of Thai cooking, it was only introduced in the late 1600s by Portuguese missionaries, who had acquired a taste for it in South America. Dutch, French and Japanese methods and ingredients were also incorporated during these years.

Many original Indian influences from the early days of Thai society have been adapted and modified. Coconut oil has replaced ghee, and potent spices have been substituted with milder varieties or with herbs.

A full, balanced Thai meal comprises a soup, a curry dish with condiments, and a dip with accompanying fish and vegetables. A spiced salad may replace the curry dish. If the soup is spicy, the curry should be replaced by non-spiced items. The idea is to create a harmony of tastes and textures across the entire meal.

The range of food available at a hawker's stall

LONELY PLANET IMAGES — RICHARD I'ANSON

History and politics

Sukhothai

Thailand has always been a fiercely independent nation. Unlike other Asian nations, it was never colonised by any of the European empires. Thai history can be traced back more than 10 000 years.

The largest grouping of Thai people was in the area of Chiang Saen, in the north of the country. These peoples were constantly under threat of invasion by the Khmers to the east. In the early thirteenth century two chieftains united to throw out the Khmer invaders. The first independent Thai kingdom was established at Sukhothai in 1238, ruled over by King Inthrathit. It was a relatively peaceful period during which many advances were made.

Most prominent of the Sukhothai kings was Ramkamhaeng, crowned in 1279. He introduced the Therava form

SUKHOTHAI
The Dawn of Happiness

of Buddhism and encouraged scholars to develop a writing system that is the basis of today's Thai script. Ramkamhaeng also expanded the kingdom considerably.

The rise of Ayutthaya

By the fourteenth century another kingdom, Ayutthaya, was on the rise. As it came to prominence, so Sukhothai declined. Ayutthaya, led by King Borom Rachathirat, absorbed Sukhothai in 1378.

The Ayutthaya kings answered to no one and were very warlike, taking the title of Devaraja, or God King. During the fifteenth century Ayutthaya expanded to the east, taking the great Khmer centre of Angkor in 1431.

A seventeenth century painting of Ayutthaya

A British East India Company ship in the Chao Praya River in the 1820s

The coming of the Europeans

By the sixteenth century explorers from Europe and Arabia were making their way to Ayutthaya. First to arrive, in 1511, were the Portuguese, who agreed to act as mercenaries and aid the kingdom in its wars. In return, the Portuguese were granted the right to trade with Ayutthaya.

Protecting the realm

King Tabinshweti of Burma invaded Ayutthaya in 1538. With Portuguese assistance, Ayutthaya repelled the attacks until 1569, finally falling to Burmese forces. Most Ayutthayan people were moved to Burma.

Fifteen-year-old Prince Naresuen escaped Burma and assembled a guerrilla army to expel the hated Burmese. He freed Ayutthaya in 1584 and repelled all attempts by the Burmese to regain the territory. In 1590 he ascended to the throne as King, or 'Naresuen the Great'.

Opening to the world

For almost 200 years Ayutthaya grew and prospered, developing into a great city. The Portuguese were followed by the Spanish in 1598. Not far behind were the Dutch, who established a trading post at Pattani in southern Thailand in 1601.

From closer to home came the Japanese, who commanded the royal bodyguards for King Song Tham (1610–28). Britain's East India Company established a trading post at Pattani in 1612. French Catholic missionaries arrived in 1662 to spread the Christian faith.

New invasions

In 1767 a reunited Burmese Empire once again took Ayutthaya, and removed vast amounts of gold and other goods. The Ayutthayan General Phya Taksin escaped to the south with a small group of supporters.

LOYALTY TO THE KING

During the reign of King Sanphet VIII (1703–09), while carrying the King down the Chao Praya River, the helmsman of the royal barge accidentally allowed it to hit the river bank. This was an act punishable by death. While the King was unperturbed, the helmsman insisted he be executed, to show respect for the law and uphold his dignity.

With a formidable army and navy, Taksin returned and expelled the Burmese. Proclaimed King, he moved the capital to Thonburi, across the river from Bangkok. Laos and Cambodia also became part of the kingdom. For around twenty years there was relative peace.

The Chakri Dynasty

When a revolt broke out among his peoples, Taksin abdicated in 1782. His replacement was General Chakri, who was crowned as King Rama I. He founded the dynasty from which the present King is descended.

To create a new symbol of unity, he moved the capital to Bangkok. Work commenced on the Wat Phra Kaew (Temple of the Emerald Buddha) and the Grand Palace.

Rama I launched wide-ranging reforms. Legal experts revamped the nation's laws, while various Buddhist practices were adapted to Siamese culture.

Expanding the kingdom

During Rama I's time, areas of lower Burma were annexed, as was Chiang Mai in the north of Siam and the Malay states of Kedah, Perlis, Kelantan and Trengganu.

Rama IV modernises

Although it lasted just seventeen years, the reign of Rama IV was one of enormous change for Siam. As well as opening up trade, King Mongkut greatly modernised his nation. Roads and canals were built, and foreign advisers upgraded government offices and the army and helped organise a police force.

General Chakri arrives back at Thonburi in 1782 following a successful campaign in Cambodia

King Mongkut, Rama IV

The Chulalongkorn era

Most of the pioneering work of Rama IV was continued by his successor, King Chulalongkorn (Rama V), who reigned from 1868 to 1910. He made history in 1897 when he travelled to Europe to shore up relations with the European powers and enhance trade opportunities. Arrangements were made for two of the king's sons to be educated in Britain.

Absolute monarchy ends

King Prajadhipok (Rama VII), who reigned from 1925 to 1934, was Siam's last absolute monarch. When the nation's rice exports collapsed during the 1930s Depression, the King ordered severe cuts in the civil service and military budgets.

These moves provoked a bloodless *coup d'état* on 24 June 1932. Led by Dr Pridi Phanomyong, a coalition of civilians and military leaders forced the King to agree to a new constitution. The new arrangements, with a European-style constitutional monarchy, came into effect on 10 December 1932. Manopakorn Nititada was the first prime minister.

More coups

Following dissent in the cabinet, there was another *coup d'état* on 20 June 1933. Manopakorn was deposed and Colonel Phanon Phomphayuhasena took his place.

Opposition to Phanon's policies resulted in a third coup on 11 October 1933, demanding a return to the absolute monarchy. This time the coup was put down in six days.

The King left Siam for Europe in 1934, reducing the chances of any attempt to re-establish an absolute monarchy. Prime Minister Phanon remained in control until 1939, when he was replaced by Pribun Songkhran.

Siam becomes Thailand

Pribun brought a distinctively military flavour to the government. He changed Siam's name to the more nationalistic Thailand (Land of

THE KING AND ANNA

King Mongkut (Rama IV) is well known as the subject of the book *Anna and the King of Siam*, written by Anna Leonowens, and the musical *The King and I*, based on the book. The widow of a British army sergeant from Singapore, Leonowens was employed by King Mongkut for five years from 1862 to teach English to his children.

The Free Thai movement was established by Dr Pridi Phanomyong, who had inspired the revolution of 1932. It was supported by, and secretly collaborated with, the Allies during the war.

Death of a king

At just twenty-two years of age, the former boy-king Ananda (Rama VIII) died in 1946. It is widely believed he was assassinated, although this has never been proved or disproved. Even today it is not discussed openly in Thai society.

the Free). Pribun was anti-Chinese and disliked the governments and ideologies of Europe and North America. The only exceptions were the fascist regimes of Hitler in Germany and Mussolini in Italy.

In 1935, when Rama VII announced his abdication, the National Assembly declared ten-year-old Prince Ananda Mahidol, son of Rama VI, to be the heir. A Council of Regents ruled in his name until he came of age.

World War II

When war was declared between the USA and Japan, Thailand allied itself with Japan and declared war on the USA and Britain. The alliance meant Thailand was spared a full-scale Japanese invasion.

It did not, however, prevent the Japanese constructing the notorious Thai–Burma railway. The track would be a link between the South China Sea and the Andaman Sea to eliminate the sea voyage around Singapore. It was built mainly by prisoners-of-war under brutal conditions.

The magnificent Chakri Palace in Bangkok

SCOTT BRODIE

Ananda's successor was his brother, Bhumibol Adulyedej, aged only eighteen years. He reigned as prince regent for four years before being crowned Rama IX.

Communism and more coups

As the communists moved to take control of China, it was widely feared the movement would sweep south into Thailand. This threat provoked the military to stage a *coup d'état* in 1947, something that would become depressingly familiar for the Thai people in decades to come.

Under military rule

Pribun was restored to the prime ministership, leading a deeply conservative government closely linked to the military. While the danger of communist take-over was averted, Thais lost many of their civil liberties.

The general election of 1957 was rigged by Pribun and his supporters, which sparked yet another military coup. Field Marshal Sarit Thanarat appointed Thanom Kittikachorn prime minister.

Less than a year later, Sarit removed Thanom and declared himself prime minister, placing Thailand under martial law.

Supporting the USA

The Sarit years (1958–1963) were a time of harsh authoritarian government. The interim constitution of 1959 made little difference to daily life. Sarit concentrated on economic growth, attracting foreign investors.

On Sarit's death in 1963 Thanom Kittikachorn returned to the leadership. He welcomed the establishment of American military bases in Thailand to support the growing war in Vietnam. In addition, large numbers of Thai soldiers were sent to serve in Vietnam.

A new constitution proclaimed in 1968 led to a period of civilian rule, although still with Thanom Kittikachorn as prime minister. Economic and political conditions worsened until, in 1971, the military staged yet another *coup d'état.*

The following year saw an economic upturn, greatly aided by the huge numbers of US military personnel being transferred to Thailand from bases in Vietnam.

Patience wears thin

By October 1973 discontent among Thai people was rife. Following a week of rioting by students in Bangkok, Thanom's government collapsed. Sanya Thammasak, a civilian, was appointed prime minister. Frustrated by lack of progress, he resigned in 1974 but was prevailed upon to continue in office. In October 1974 a new constitution was introduced.

Back to military rule

For two years Thailand was under civilian rule until, in 1976, another coup brought Thailand back under military control. General Kriangsak Chamanand held the prime ministership until he was replaced in 1980 by General Prem Tinsulanond.

Prem defeated two coups before resigning after the elections of July 1988. His place was taken by Chart Thai party leader, Major-General Chatichai Choonhaven.

In the 1970s, after the war in Vietnam had ended, hundreds of thousands of refugees streamed into Thailand. Pol Pot's murderous Khmer Rouge made the eastern jungles of Thailand its base after being driven out of Cambodia.

The people act

Under military rule, Thailand prospered economically through the 1980s. However, Thais were far from happy with their government and lack of democracy. In February 1991, in another coup, government leaders were arrested and the constitution was suspended.

A new and much-criticised constitution was introduced in late 1991 and elections were held in March 1992. Although not elected, General Suchinda Kraprayoon was named prime minister.

The people were outraged. Several prominent politicians went on hunger strikes. Following mass rallies of hundreds of thousands of demonstrators, reforms were announced.

Thai traditional dress

SCOTT BRODIE

However, when nothing more happened, demonstrations erupted once again. During the ensuing state of emergency, on 18 May, police killed more than a hundred demonstrators and arrested 3000.

The subsequent turmoil and criticism forced King Bhumibol to act. He negotiated a settlement that reinstated civilian government. At new elections held in September 1992, anti-military parties won control of the government. The new prime minister, Chuan Leekpai, headed a coalition of parties.

A time of change

Thailand saw considerable advancements over the next three years. The new constitution of January 1995 lowered the voting age to eighteen, granted equal rights to women, and reduced the influence of the military. Unfortunately, six months later, after being rocked by a land-reform scandal, the Chuan government collapsed.

Chuan was replaced by a coalition led by Banharn Silpa-archa. He lasted barely eighteen months before being replaced by Chavalit Yongchaiyudh. Chavalit, in turn, resigned in November 1997, handing the prime ministership back to Chuan Leekpai. Another new constitution was proclaimed in September.

The economic collapse

All through the 1990s Thailand was hailed as one of the Asian 'tiger' economies. However, the economic strength proved to be an illusion.

Many years of government corruption and overvalued property markets resulted in the collapse of the baht, Thailand's currency, in July 1997. It sparked a major crisis across Asia, with one country after another suffering rapid economic slowdowns. In Thailand thousands were thrown out of work and many lost millions in the collapse. The International Monetary Fund's US$17 billion recovery package ensured that, within two years, Thailand was once more experiencing growth.

The suffering and confusion of the people were reflected in the results of the January 2001 elections. Chuan Leekpai's government was defeated by a coalition of the Thai Rak Tai (TRT), Chart Thai and Kwam Wang Mai parties. Thaksin Shinawatra, a wealthy businessman and leader of the TRT, became prime minister.

WWW.SOURCES

www.sala.net/Thailand/history.html
General history of Thailand

sunsite.au.ac.th/thailand/thai_his/
Thai history

www.asianinfo.org/asianinfo/thailand/politics.htm
Politics in Thailand

Statistics

Total population
61 797 751
Birth rate
16.6 per 1000 population
Death rate
7.5 per 1000 population
Infant mortality rate
30 per 1000 live births
Life expectancy
male 65, female 72

GDP growth rate   4.2%
GDP per capita   US$6700
GDP by sector
agriculture 13%
industry 40%
services 47%
Population below
poverty line   12.5%
Government revenues
US$19 billion
Government expenditures
US$21 billion

Labour force   32.6 million
Labour force by sector
agriculture 54%
industry 15%
services 31%
Unemployment rate   4%

Land area
513 115 sq. km
Lowest point
Gulf of Thailand — sea level
Highest point
Doi Inthanon — 2576 m
Natural resources
Tin, rubber, natural gas, tungsten,
tantalum, timber, lead, fish,
gypsum, lignite, fluorite

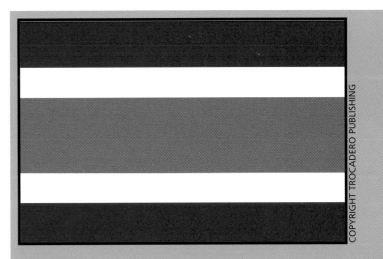

Thailand's flag is called Trairanga, which means tricolour. It was adopted in September 1917. The red colour symbolises the blood shed by the people to protect Thailand; the white symbolises the purity of the Buddhist religion; and the blue symbolises the monarchy.

Principal crops
rice, cassava (tapioca),
rubber, corn, sugar cane,
coconuts, soybeans

Secondary industries
tourism, textiles and garments,
agricultural processing,
beverages, cement, light
manufacturing, electrical
appliances and components,
computers and parts, integrated
circuits, furniture, plastics

Major exports
Computers and components,
clothing and textiles, rice

Official language   Thai
Currency   Thai baht
Religions   Buddhism, Islam

Index

Focus on Asia: Thailand   ISBN 0 86415 429 1
Published by   Franklin Watts 96 Leonard Street London EC2A4XD
Created and produced by Trocadero Publishing   Copyright © 2002 S and L Brodie   Printed in Hong Kong